TM 11-380

M-209 CONVERTER ENCRYPTION MACHINE TECHNICAL MANUAL

by WAR DEPARTMENT

April 27, 1942

RESTRICTED

TECHNICAL MANUAL }
No. 11-380

WAR DEPARTMENT,
WASHINGTON, *April 27, 1942.*

CONVERTER M-209

Prepared under direction of the
Chief Signal Officer

SIGNAL CORPS

TABLE OF CONTENTS

CONVERTER M-209

Section I

GENERAL

1. **Purpose and distribution.**—*a*. Converter M-209 is an item of equipment issued by the Signal Corps for use by such holders as may be designated by the Chief Signal Officer.

b. The instructions contained herein are applicable to all cryptographic systems employing Converter M-209 except as they may be modified by the Cipher Key Lists employed with a particular system.

2. **Description.**—*a*. Converter M-209 is a small, compact, hand-operated, tape-printing, mechanical device designed for rapid encipherment and decipherment of tactical messages which must be cryptographed before transmission. It is normally carried in a canvas case on a strap over the shoulder. The carrying strap may be attached underneath

the machine for securing it to the knee of the operator when used in the field or in a moving vehicle. A hand strap is also provided which may be attached to the left side of the machine. The case has compartments for carrying this technical manual, pencils, extra tape, message blanks, etc.

b. The cryptographic principle upon which the M-209 operates is that of reciprocal substitution alphabets. The effect is that of sliding a normal-alphabet sequence against the same sequence reversed. A high degree of irregularity in the shifting of the alphabets with respect to each other is brought about by a train of gears in which the number of teeth on the driving member is varied under the influence of certain keying elements to be described in subsequent paragraphs.

c. Identification of parts.—The following numbered list in connection with the photographs shown on pages 33 and 34 will serve to identify the various parts of the Converter M-209 as they are referred to in these instructions:

1. Letter counter window	9. Encipher-decipher knob
2. Letter counter	10. Reading window
3. Indicating index	11. Paper feed knob
4. Ink pad	12. Paper tape
5. Type wheel	13. Paper pressure arm
6. Reproducing disk	14. Cover support
7. Indicating disk	15. Ink pad container
8. Setting knob	16. Screw-driver

17. Oil can	28. Number ring
18. Outer cover	29. Drum bar
19. Catch for inner lid	30. Drum bar lug
20. Cover catch button	31. Inter-lock lever
21. Paper guard catch	32. Drive knob
22. Paper guard	33. Reset knob
23. Paper roll	34. Key wheel bench mark
24. Tweezers	35. Ineffective pin
25. Reset button	36. Effective pin
26. Inner lid	37. Key wheels
27. Number plate	

d. The outer cover (18)* of the machine may be opened by pushing in on the knob (20) which is centrally located in the front. The cover being opened, the machine is seen to consist principally of the following:

(1) A series of six *key wheels* (37), bearing letters on their peripheries and showing through apertures in the inner lid (26) of the device.

(2) A large knurled knob at the left (8) attached to a metal disk (7), called the *indicating disk,* bearing the letters of the alphabet in normal order. The indicating disk is associated with a reproducing disk (6), one letter of which is visible through aperture (10).

---

*See photographs pages 33-34.

(3) A small knurled knob (11), *the paper feed knob,* directly behind the indicating disk. This knob can be turned only towards the rear of the machine and with its associated roller, the tape advancing roller, advances the paper tape (12), on which printing is effected by operating the machine.

(4) A cutting edge, at which the paper tape may be torn off in a clean manner when so desired.

(5) A window (1), at the front left-hand corner of the inner lid (26), through which a letter counter (2), is visible.

(6) A knurled knob (33), on the right-hand side of the machine, which can be turned only by simultaneously depressing the button (25) at the back right-hand corner of the inner lid, whereupon the key wheels are rotatable as a unit, forward or backward, and the letter counter is operated correspondingly.

(7) An encipher-decipher knob (9) just below the paper feed knob (11).

(8) A drive knob (32) at the right-hand side of the device.

3. **Miscellaneous information.**—*a. Paper tape supply.*— To insert a fresh tape into the feed mechanism, the hinged

guard (22) which holds the paper in place should be released and allowed to tilt forward against the inner lid. The empty spool should be removed and a new roll of tape placed over the pin so that it will unroll in a counter-clockwise direction. The end of the tape should be passed through the slot in the guard and brought forward and inserted in the tape slot just above the encipher-decipher knob (9). Push the tape through the tape channel until it appears at the top, making certain that the paper passes under the two small springs immediately behind the type wheel (5); then pass it between the tape-advancing rollers while pressing downward on the paper pressure arm (13).

b. Inking Pad and Type Wheel.—(1) Extra inking pads will be found in one of the small metal containers held by spring clips in the outer cover of the machine. To insert a fresh pad, open the inner lid (26), remove the old pad by means of the tweezers, and insert a new one in its place. The life of a pad can be prolonged by turning it end for end.

(2) After considerable use the type wheel (5) may become caked with ink and will produce indistinct characters. The type wheel assembly may be removed by loosening the screw inside the setting knob (8). The type is cleaned, as on a typewriter, with type cleaner and a typewriter brush.

c. Oiling.—Where oil holes are provided for lubricating bearings a drop of oil should be inserted occasionally from the container in the cover. Except as regards the left end of the drum, which should be kept well oiled, all other points where friction occurs should be oiled only sparingly from time to time. *Excessive oiling must be avoided.*

d. When paper or ink supply is exhausted.—If the printing becomes illegible or fails to function due to exhaustion of the paper tape reserve or ink supply, the cipher text or clear text can be read off the letters on the reproducing disk (6) when these appear in the aperture (10) *after* each manipulation of the operating lever.

e. Repairs.—Should defective or worn parts cause trouble no attempt should be made to effect repairs locally except those of a very minor nature, such as replacement of a broken or disconnected spring. The machine should be returned through channels to the issuing office in order that proper steps may be taken either to repair the machine or to replace it with a serviceable one.

Section II

CIPHER KEYS AND KEY LISTS

4. **Cryptographic Systems.**—A cryptographic system employing one of these machines consists of:

(1) The Converter M-209.

(2) This manual (TM 11-380), which contains operating instructions for the M-209.

(3) Publications called *Cipher Key Lists,* issued periodically, containing instructions governing the arrangement of the keying elements for the system. Instructions for the preparation of Cipher Key Lists will be found in paragraph 8.

5. **Necessity for keys and changes therein.**—*a.* In order that holders of Converter M-209 may communicate with one

another, it is necessary that the cryptographic mechanisms of their devices be set to identical initial positions and that these mechanisms progress in an absolutely identical manner from these initial positions. This is accomplished by setting the elements of the cryptographic mechanisms to definite positions and adjustments according to a *cipher key* applicable to a set of *keying elements* which are described in paragraph 6.

b. While the machine possesses a high degree of cryptographic security, it is still not absolutely invulnerable to solution, especially if a large volume of traffic is allowed to be enciphered by means of any one arrangement of the keying elements. The length of time a given arrangement will resist solution depends upon a number of variable factors, but in order to provide maximum security, changes of cipher keys should be effected at very frequent intervals. A daily change in the keying elements referred to below as the "internal keying elements" would not be too frequent, while the "external keying element" should be different for every message. The method of determining or indicating the changes in the arrangement of the keying elements must be agreed upon in advance and thoroughly understood by all who are to use the machine.

6. **Keying elements.** — The keying elements for the M-209 are three in number and are divided into two groups:

a. The external keying element.—This element of the key is the one determined and selected by the operator himself and will be different for every message enciphered. It refers to the initial alignment of the six key wheels (37) as indicated by a series of letters which are lined up from left to right along the white bench mark (34). This series of letters, in one form or another, will appear in the message as the message indicator referred to in paragraph 7 below.

b. The internal keying elements.—These elements of the key are two in number and they are to be changed only as directed by the signal or communication officer of the unit concerned. They refer to, *1st*, the number of effective pins (36) in each of the six key wheels, and, *2d*, the positions of the movable lugs (30) on the drum bars (29). Detailed instructions for the arrangement of both sets of keying elements are given in paragraph 9.

7. **Indicators**.—Every cryptogram enciphered by means of the M-209 will have both a *system indicator* and a *message indicator*. The system indicator will be found in a publication describing the particular system involved, or will be provided for in Signal Operation Instructions. It will appear in the message immediately following the writer's number

group, if any. It will also appear at the end of the message before the writer's time, if any. The message indicator is selected by the operator himself and determines for each message the initial positions of the six key wheels. It will appear in the message immediately after the first appearance and immediately before the second appearance of the system indicator. In choosing a message indicator the operator writes down a random selection of five letters, subject to the limitations of the letters actually present on the key wheels. Since the first of these five letters governs the setting of the first two wheels, counting from left to right, any letter from A to Z, except W, can be used as the first letter of the indicator. For the second letter, governing wheel number 3, the choice ranges from A to X, omitting W. For wheel number 4 (third letter) any letter from A to U may be selected, for wheel number 5 (fourth letter) any letter from A to S, and for wheel number 6 (fifth letter) any letter from A to Q. An example of such a message indicator would be HILQD and the wheels would be adjusted so that the letters HHILQD would be lined up along the bench mark. Additional security may be obtained by enciphering the message indicator in accordance with instructions contained in the appropriate Cipher Key List.

8. **Preparation of Cipher Key Lists.**—*a*. In order that

Signal Operation Instructions may indicate in an absolutely clear and unambiguous manner the arrangement of the internal keying elements, it is essential that definite forms and procedures be followed in preparing the Cipher Key Lists.

b. To prepare a table of pin settings which will have a favorable randomizing effect on the shifting of the alphabets proceed as follows:

(1) Prepare a chart of the key wheels by listing in alphabetical order, starting with A, the letters appearing on the face of each wheel: the first wheel, A to Z, the second wheel A to Z omitting W, the third wheel A to X omitting W, the fourth wheel A to U, the fifth wheel A to S, and the sixth wheel A to Q.

(2) Prepare a set of 156 lettered cards or counters, 78 of which are marked R and the remainder L. Shuffle the cards or counters thoroughly and draw out one at a time, marking with a dash the position of the pins successively, starting with A on wheel number 1, in accordance with the letter drawn: if R, make a dash to the right of the letter, if L, make a dash to the left. (See sample table on page 17). This procedure insures a perfectly random assortment in which from 40 to 60 per cent of the pins are in the effective position.

c. To prepare a table of favorable settings for the drum bar lugs proceed as follows:

(1) Mark off six columns of ¼-inch cross-section paper and number the columns from 1 to 6. These numbers denote the effective positions for lug settings. Number the rows of the form from 1 to 27, starting at the top. These numbers denote the drum bars in the order in which they become effective during an operating cycle of the machine.

(2) Select any set of six numbers, subject to the following limitations:

(a) Their sum must not be less than 28 nor more than 39;

(b) Three of the numbers should be odd and three even;

(c) No one number should be greater than 13;

(d) There should be a more or less uniform progression from the lowest to the highest number;

(e) The numbers must be so selected that the various combinations of one or more will, when added together, yield all the numbers from 1 to 27, inclusive, bearing in mind that the effect of two effective lugs on the same drum bar is 1. For example, the numbers 4 and 8 in columns 4 and 5, respectively, of Table 2 below total 11, not 12, because there are two effective lugs on bar number 10.

An example of such a set of numbers is 1, 2, 3, 4, 8, 11.

The foregoing limitations are imposed to prevent any tendencies toward monoalphabeticity in the shifting of the alphabets, and to add to the difficulties of enemy cryptanalysts in making a mathematical analysis of the messages.

(3) The numbers are now inserted in the chart in such a manner as to indicate the number of effective lugs, in each position from 1 to 6, on the bars forming the drum bar cage. Make an X in cell 1 of column 1, in cells 2 and 3 of column 2, in cells 4-6 of column 3, in cells 7-10 of column 4, in cells 10-17 of column 5, and in cells 17-27 of column 6. (See sample Table 2, below). Each X denotes the position of an effective lug. Unused lugs are left in the zero or ineffective position. The columns of the chart can be transposed in any order to form additional keys which may all be used. It is preferable, however, not to use such keys in succession, but to space their use over several weeks.

d. Having prepared the tables of settings for both the key wheel pins and the drum bar lugs, it is desirable to provide a means by which holders of the machine can check the accuracy of their settings. This is done by adjusting the machine in accordance with the charts and enciphering the letter A twenty-six times, starting with the key wheels aligned on the letters AAAAAA. The twenty-six cipher equivalents are included with the two tables as a check, so that, having made his adjustments, the holder of a machine may test their accuracy by himself enciphering twenty-six A's with the key wheels set initially at AAAAAA. Any deviation from the 26-letter check indicates that an error was made in the settings and necessitates a recheck of the entire adjustment. The 26-letter check should be derived for and included with every pair of keying tables issued and will be given in the Cipher Key List merely as a sequence of letters such as the following:

26-letter check

T K H R X C U Y T K N O I K R J N T A D T A I V P M

c. An example of the form in which the two tables referred to in subparagraphs b and c above will appear in the Cipher Key Lists is shown in Tables 1 and 2 on pp. 17-18. In Table 1, "A—" indicates that the pin designated by the letter A on the key wheel in question is to be pushed to the right, while "—A" indicates that the pin designated by the letter A is to be placed in the left position. In Table 2 it is indicated that the left-hand lug on bar number 1 (see number ring (28)) is in the number 1 position, the left-hand lug on bars number 2 and 3 are in the number 2 position, etc. The zero positions are not shown on the table since it is obvious that a lug not in one of the numbered positions must be in a zero position. These positions are determined by reference to the number plate (27) at the rear of the drum bar cage.

16

TABLE 1—*Position of Key Wheel Pins*
Period of (date) to (date)

No. 1 (26)	No. 2 (25)	No. 3 (23)	No. 4 (21)	No. 5 (19)	No. 6 (17)
A—	—A	A—	—A	—A	A—
B—	—B	B—	—B	B—	B—
—C	—C	—C	C—	—C	—C
D—	D—	—D	—D	D—	D—
—E	E—	—E	E—	E—	—E
—F	—F	—F	F—	F—	—F
—G	G—	G—	—G	—G	—G
H—	—H	H—	H—	H—	H—
I—	—I	—I	I—	I—	—I
—J	J—	J—	—J	—J	—J
K—	K—	—K	—K	—K	K—
—L	L—	L—	—L	—L	—L
M—	—M	M—	M—	M—	—M
N—	—N	N—	N—	N—	N—
—O	O—	—O	—O	—O	O—
—P	—P	—P	P—	P—	—P
—Q	—Q	—Q	—Q	—Q	Q—
—R	R—	R—	—R	—R	
S—	S—	S—	S—	S—	
T—	—T	T—	T—		
—U	U—	U—	U—		
V—	—V	V—			
W—	X—	X—			
—X	—Y				
—Y	—Z				
—Z					

17

TABLE 2—*Position of Drum Bar Lugs*
Period of (date) to (date)

	1	2	3	4	5	6
1	X					
2		X				
3		X				
4			X			
5			X			
6			X			
7				X		
8				X		
9				X		
10				X	X	
11					X	
12					X	
13					X	
14					X	
15					X	
16					X	
17					X	X
18						X
19						X
20						X
21						X
22						X
23						X
24						X
25						X
26						X
27						X

Section III

OPERATING PROCEDURE

9. **Setting up the keying elements.**—*a. The internal keying elements.*—As stated in paragraph 6, the internal keying elements are two in number and are governed by a Cipher Key List similar to that described in paragraph 8.

(1) *Key wheel pins.*—Each of the six key wheels carries near its periphery a number (equal to the number of letters on the key wheel) of equally-spaced pins which are somewhat longer than the thickness of the wheel. These pins can be pushed to left or right by hand or by means of a knife blade or other thin instrument such as the special screwdriver (16) which is found inside the outer cover of the

19

machine. When pushed to the right the pins are in such a position that guide arms are permitted to move the drum bars (29), which, in turn, advance the type wheel through the train of gears mentioned in paragraph 2*b*. This is called the *effective* position of the pins. Pushed to the left the pins are in their *non-effective* position, i.e. they are in such a position that the guide arms are prevented from moving the drum bars. When pins are pushed to the right their left ends must be flush with the left-hand side of the key wheel, and when pushed to the left their right ends must be flush with the right-hand side of the key wheel; *intermediate positions will give faulty results when enciphering or deciphering.* When the pins on all the wheels are *all* in either their effective or non-effective positions, the resulting encipherment will be monoalphabetic. This must be avoided. From 40 to 60 per cent of the pins should be in their effective positions.

(2) *Drum bar lugs.*—There are 27 drum bars (29), arranged about a central shaft, forming a sort of basket or cage at the back of the machine. Each of these drum bars is equipped with two movable lugs, either of which causes the drum bar to move to the left when actuated by a guide arm which, in turn, is permitted to operate by an effective pin on one of the key wheels. Each drum bar has eight holes at which the two movable lugs may be located by means of the

special screw-driver (16) provided for that purpose. Two of
the holes are marked with a zero, and the others from 1 to
6, on the scale at the back of the machine. When a drum bar
lug is in the zero position, it is not actuated at all, although
the drum bar to which it is attached may still be moved if
the other lug is not also in a zero position. When a lug is in
any one of the positions 1 to 6, inclusive, the drum bar to
which it is attached will be actuated by the corresponding
key wheel whenever one of its effective pins permits one of
the drum bar activating guide arms to be depressed. When
moving the lugs into their prescribed positions, push them
with the aid of the notched screw-driver slightly toward the
front of the machine in order to disengage them from the
hole in the drum bar. Be sure that the lugs "snap" into the
desired positions, as lugs only slightly out of proper adjustment will not only produce faulty texts but may also cause
jamming of the machine. In order to facilitate proper lug
settings and the checking thereof, it is recommended that the
left-hand lugs be placed only in positions 1, 2, 3, and the
left zero, while the right-hand lugs are used in positions 4,
5, 6 and the right zero.

b. The external keying element.—This element of the key,
as stated in paragraph 6, refers to the initial alignment of
the six key wheels in accordance with a series of letters

chosen at random by the operator and appearing in the message as the message indicator (paragraph 7). In order to set the key wheels to their initial positions as indicated by the letters of the message indicator, proceed as follows:

(1) Test the drive knob (32) to ascertain that it is in a locked position. It automatically assumes this position at the end of each operating cycle, that is, after a letter has been printed on the tape and the drive knob is returned to its initial position. *THE DRIVE KNOB CANNOT BE MOVED AGAIN UNTIL AFTER THE INDICATING DISK IS MOVED.* The drive knob must remain in the locked position until all adjustments have been made.

(2) The letter counter must be set to zero. This is accomplished by turning the knob (33) while the button (25) is depressed. The reason for this step is two-fold. First, it will insure that in encipherment the first character printed will be the initial letter of a 5-letter group, so that the cryptographic text will be correctly grouped in 5's when the message has been completed. Second, the counter will show the exact number of letters enciphered or deciphered, which will be of considerable value in checking.

(3) The key wheels are now set to the letters of the message indicator by turning each wheel individually until the

desired letter is aligned on the white *bench mark* (34) across the slots through which the key wheels protrude. Since the wheels turn in only one direction, care must be taken not to turn the desired letter beyond the bench mark. The flat end of the tweezers may be used for turning the key wheels. *Eraser tips must not be used for this purpose.*

10. **Encipherment.**—The internal keying elements of the machine having been adjusted as directed in Signal Operation Instructions and in accordance with instructions contained in the preceding paragraph, the operator selects a message indicator and adjusts the key wheels in accordance therewith (See paragraph 7). To encipher a message proceed as follows:

a. Turn the encipher-decipher knob (9) so that the letter "C" is upward. This sets the machine for enciphering.

b. Advance the paper tape so as to leave about 6 inches of space before the first letter is printed. This space is for the insertion, by hand, of the address, signature, message number, and message indicator.

c. The letters of the text are located on the indicating disk and brought, one after another, to register with the indicating index or bench mark (3) by turning the indicating disk knob accordingly. *After each adjustment the fingers must be*

23

*removed from the indicating disk knob and the drive knob
turned through a complete cycle.* The cipher text will be
printed and automatically spaced in 5-letter groups on the
paper tape (12) during these operations. If the letter Z on
the indicating disk is used as a space sign after each word,
the message on decipherment will automatically be spaced
into correct word lengths of the original plain-text. *In the
event that a desired letter on the indicating disk is already
in register with the index, it is necessary to move the indicating disk slightly and return the letter to registration before
the drive knob can be moved.* After the message has been
enciphered, advance the tape by turning the knob (11) until
the printing moves out at least six inches beyond the cutting
edge, and tear off the tape.

d. Now write at the head of the tape the address, writer's
message number, date of message, and any other necessary
transmitting data. Follow this by the system and message
indicators (as two 5-letter groups). At the end of the tape,
repeat the message and system indicators (in that order)
and add the time of signature. The tape may then be handed
in that form to the transmitting operator, or it may be
pasted on a message blank.

11. **Decipherment.**—The internal keying elements hav-

24

ing been adjusted as for encipherment (paragraph 10), to decipher a message, proceed as follows:

a. Turn the encipher-decipher knob so that the letter "D" is upward. This sets the machine for deciphering.

b. Set the letter counter to zero.

c. Set the key wheels to the message indicator (the second group of the message proper). Check these letters against the second appearance of the indicator at the end of the cryptogram.

d. Operate the machine as in encipherment bringing the successive letters of the cipher text to the bench mark, by turning the indicating disk. *The spaces between the 5-letter groups of the cipher text are disregarded.* The plain-text on the tape may be copied upon a message blank or the tape may be pasted directly thereon for delivery to the addressee.

12. **Automatic spacing and the letter Z.**—It was noted in subparagraph 10*c* that in encipherment the cryptographic text is automatically printed in 5-letter groups, and that if in this process the letter Z is enciphered as the space sign between successive words, on decipherment the plain-text will be automatically reproduced in its original word lengths. This is possible only at the expense of eliminating Z as one

25

of the letters of the alphabet. If a word containing the letter Z occurs in the plain-text of a message to be enciphered, for example, the word ORGANIZED, on decipherment the text will be reproduced as ORGANI ED, but the missing letter can of course be supplied by the context.

13. **Checking and correcting errors.**—If in the course of decipherment the operator wishes to go back and check or correct a word, he can do so very easily by proceeding as follows:

a. Ascertain the position of the last letter or letters which are correct, counting from the first cipher letter. For example, if the operator wishes to go back to the beginning of the 25th group in the message, the 1st letter of that group is $(24 \times 5) + 1 = 121$st letter. Since the counter showed zero at the beginning of decipherment and is now at say 129, the operator must reset the key wheels to the position they occupied after the encipherment of the 120th letter. He depresses button (25), and revolves reset knob (33) until the stroke counter reads 120. The machine is now ready to decipher the 121st letter of the message, that is, the first letter of the 25th group. The procedure is the same if the operator has been disturbed and has lost his place in the message he is deciphering.

26

b. If in the course of encipherment the operator wishes to go back to correct or change a word, the procedure is the same as above except that much more care is necessary to find the numerical position of the letters or letter he wishes to correct, since he must refer to his plain text, count the letters in each word, and also count the spaces between words if he has used Z to separate them in encipherment.

14. **Defective operation.**—*a.* Although Converter M-209 is ruggedly constructed, it must nevertheless be handled with due care to assure satisfactory operation. Excessive speed in moving the drive knob should be avoided. A steady, moderate, smooth operation will give the best results.

b. Each operating cycle must be *fully* completed before attempting to set the indicating disk to the next letter; likewise, before attempting to move the drive knob after a preceding complete cycle, the indicating disk must be moved, even if it happens then to be set at the letter desired. Also, be sure that the reset knob (33) at the right of the machine is in a locked position. It will click slightly when the key wheels, if rotated together, come in alignment with the white bench mark and the counter shows its figures properly. It should be noted that the knob (33) operates an inter-lock lever (31) (See Fig. 2). This inter-lock lever allows the reset knob (33) to be operated only when the drum bar cage is in its starting position (which is at the same time its final position, on completion of the operating cycle). Also if the reset knob has not "clicked" into position, it will be found that the cage will be locked, the lever (31) engaging with a notch in the number ring (28). If the key wheels have been turned individually, be sure that each wheel has "clicked" into position with the desired letter registering with the white bench mark, because if the wheel is not quite in position, there may be an error in the first text letter. All above-mentioned members are interlocked in a way that will insure correct operation, but if a movement is not completed or if one of the cited members is left in an intermediate or incorrect position and an attempt is made to move the drive knob, the result is likely to be a "jamming" of the operating mechanism. *If this should occur, never use force in an attempt to eliminate or overcome the trouble and thus "clear" the mechanism.* First, try to locate the cause of the jamming and if it cannot be traced back to such faults as incomplete movements or faulty positioning of the operating members, it may have been caused by excessive speed in moving the drive knob. To clear a jam of the latter type, open the inner lid of the machine, and rock the drum bar cage back and forth, unless the movement can be completed by means of the drive knob.

c. Another cause of jamming is incorrect positioning of the lugs on the drum bars. Each drum bar, if activated, should move out the same distance to the left of the drum as other active bars. Failure to move out properly is caused by a lug not being in proper position. To relieve a jam due to this cause, locate the improperly-positioned lug (usually bearing against the end of one of the drum bar activating guide arms) and move it to the proper position by means of the special screw-driver.

d. In all respects the most important safeguard against faulty operation, either mechanical or cryptographic, is the following: *Complete every necessary movement; make sure that operating members are accurately positioned and are not in intermediate positions.*

15. **Destruction of Converter M-209.**—In case it should become necessary to destroy the converter because of imminent danger of capture by the enemy or for any other reason, the destruction will be accomplished in the following manner. First, see that all keying elements are in neutral positions by changing all lug settings to zero and moving all key wheel pins to the left position. Second, see that the machine is rendered unserviceable to the enemy by stamping upon it with a boot heel or by firing into it with a rifle or pistol.

29

16. **Parts list.**—The following is a list of parts of the Converter M-209 which are most readily replaceable in case of necessity. A complete list will be found in the Signal Corps Catalog.

Quantity	Nomenclature	Mfr's Part No.	Photograph Ref. No.
4	Foot, rubber	R2	
4	Screw, foot, rubber	R4	
4	Screw, sideplate, right-hand	R17	
2	Screw, sideplate, left-hand	R17	
4	Screw, lid hinge	R38	
4	Lock washer, lid hinge	R39	
4	Screw, cover hinge	R38	
1	Support, cover	R63	14
1	Hub, cover support	R64	
1	Spring, cover support	R65	
1	Screw, cover support	R66	
2	Holder, oil can	R82	
4	Screw, oil can holder	R83	
1	Latchplate, cover	R92	
2	Screw, latchplate, cover	R92A	
1	Screw, set, key wheel shaft	R117	
2	Screw, end, key wheel shaft	R118	
1	Knob, key wheel reset	R132	33
2	Screw, intermediate gear shaft bearing	R173	
1	Spring, intermediate gear release arm	R195	

Quantity	Nomenclature	Mfr's Part No.	Photo-graph Ref. No.
1	Knob, drive (operating lever)	R230	32
1	Cotter, drive knob	R232	
1	Type wheel	R240	5
1	Band, type wheel	R240A	
1	Pin, type wheel band	R240B	
1	Arm, ink pad	MR262	
1	Bracket, ink pad arm	MR264	
1	Spring arm, ink pad	MR266	
2	Screw, ink pad arm bracket	R265	
2	Lock washer, ink pad arm bracket	R265A	
1	Hammer, print arm	R277.	
1	Rubber, print arm hammer	R278	
1	Screw, print arm hammer	R279	
1	Ball, encipher-decipher knob detent	R297	
1	Spring, knob detent	R298	
1	Screw, knob detent	R299	
1	Spring, paper feed cam	R303	
1	Spring, paper feed pawl	R307	
1	Knob, paper feed	R314	11
1	Cotter, paper feed knob	R315	
1	Spring, paper pressure arm	R325	
1	Counter	R340	
1	Gear, counter	R341	
1	Cotter, counter gear	R342	
2	Screw, counter	R346	
2	Lock washer, counter	R347	

Quantity	Nomenclature	Mfr's Part No.	Photo-graph Ref. No.
1	Tweezers	R350	24
1	Screw-driver	R351	16
1	Oil can	MR352	17
1	Oil can cover	MR354	
1	Ink pad can	MR358	15
1	Ink pad can cover	MR359	
6	Ink pad, complete with bushing	MR357	
1	Paper roll	R360	23
1	Case, canvas, (complete with strap)		
1	Strap, hand, carrying (complete with snaps)		

[A.G. 062.11 (5-28-42)]

BY ORDER OF THE SECRETARY OF WAR:

G. C. MARSHALL,

Chief of Staff.

OFFICIAL:

J. A. ULIO,

Major General,

The Adjutant General.

DISTRIBUTION:

IBn & H 1 and 8 (2); IC and H 1, 2, 4, 6, and 7, (2), 11 (8), and 17 (3).

(For explanation of symbols see FM 21-6.)

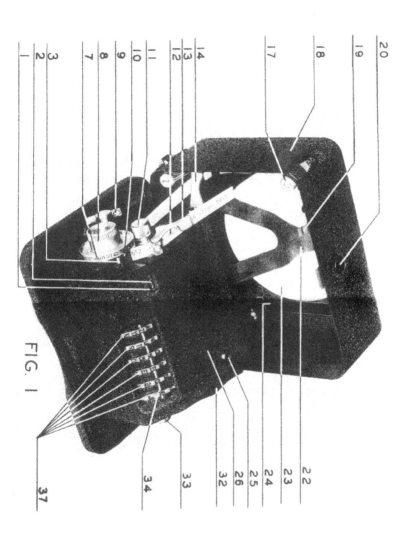

FIG. 1

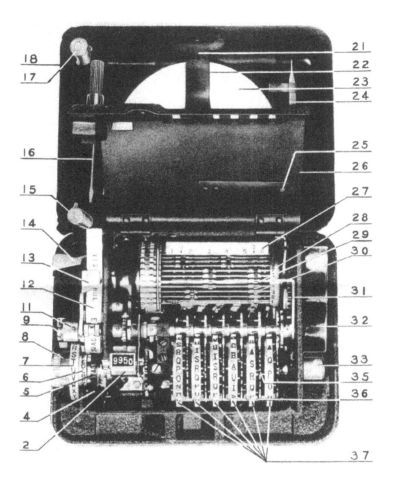

FIG. 2

34